What I Have
Heard in Silence

What I Have Heard in Silence

A Workbook for Entering the Kingdom of Heaven

SAM V. CHIARELLA

WHAT I HAVE HEARD IN SILENCE
A WORKBOOK FOR ENTERING THE KINGDOM OF HEAVEN

iUniverse books may be ordered through booksellers or by contacting:

iUniverse
1663 Liberty Drive
Bloomington, IN 47403
www.iuniverse.com
1-800-Authors (1-800-288-4677)

Because of the dynamic nature of the Internet, any web addresses or links contained in this book may have changed since publication and may no longer be valid. The views expressed in this work are solely those of the author and do not necessarily reflect the views of the publisher, and the publisher hereby disclaims any responsibility for them.

Any people depicted in stock imagery provided by Thinkstock are models, and such images are being used for illustrative purposes only.
Certain stock imagery © Thinkstock.

ISBN: 978-1-4917-9399-2 (sc)
ISBN: 978-1-4917-9400-5 (e)

Print information available on the last page.

iUniverse rev. date: 4/29/2016

TO MAE BETH, ADAM AND JASON
WHO COMPLETE MY PERFECT FOURSOME FOR HEAVEN

Contents

Preface:
How This Book Came to Be Written

This book came to be written while I was in church at what Catholics call "Eucharistic Adoration". This is where the priest exposes the consecrated Body of Christ usually in front of a tabernacle in church, and people come to pray and worship God through His Son, Jesus. This is done on special occasions, or on one day per week or month, or even "perpetually" in some parishes, which means that it is done twenty-four hours per day, seven days per week.

Parishioners sign up to come and pray for thirty minutes or one hour at a time. Each person then repeats his or her time every week, or once per month, as in *Nocturnal Adoration* which is done on the first Friday and Saturday of every month. You come to pray and ask God for your needs, and those needs of friends and family members. You also come to thank God for all of your blessings. It is an extraordinary time of peace and asking for forgiveness of sins or just having a talk with God, His Son Jesus, or the Holy Spirit.

As I was praying and meditating during one Adoration time, I heard a voice say: "Write this down". I had brought a pen and notebook to remind me of some of the people and things that I wanted to pray for. So I started hearing sentences, and I wrote down two or three pages as fast as I possibly could. I did not hear a direct voice as you would when talking to someone, but I knew exactly what to write down. It was more like "contemplative prayer", which is praying in silence from your heart. I continued coming to adoration with a pen and paper in hand, and I just started writing the words that came to me. These words came quickly and effortlessly, and I believe that they were not originated by me, since I usually struggle when writing a speech or an essay.

I believe that God is using me as a messenger to spread this information to you, and anyone that you choose to give a copy of this book to. *Please keep your copy of the book and notes to review and add new thoughts to the topics as you see fit.* Just like a fine automobile, we all need a *tune-up* every now and then, just to keep our lives running a little more smoothly.

NOTE 1: All bible quotes are from the New Revised Standard Version Bible: Catholic Edition copyright 1989, 1993 the Division of Christian Education of the National Council of the Churches of Christ in the United States of America. Used by permission. All rights reserved. See also <u>biblegateway.com</u>

<u>NOTE 2</u>: Fifteen stories with the author's name and city were written by friends of mine. I asked each friend to recall a special event in his or her life that had sparked or increased their faith. Most of us have had something happen that we will never forget. We may have never written it down, but we carry it with us every day. The other fifteen stories with no author's name or city were written by me --- Sam V. Chiarella. I hope that you enjoy all thirty short stories, and that you might share your own story with others some day.

How To Use This Workbook

Let this workbook be: an examination of your conscience, a roadmap, a prayer, but most of all a gift from God. He wants you to be with Him, so that He can shower you with His infinite love and peace.

In order to get the most out of this book, I suggest that you use the following steps:

1) Take ten to fifteen minutes at the beginning of your week to do some reading and planning.

2) Work on only one topic per week, in order or whichever topic you wish. (There are twenty-six topics, so you can concentrate on one per week, and cover them all *twice* in one year.)

3) Read the brief scripture page and then the following short story.

4) Then read the messages on the topic page, and underline words or phrases that seem to speak to you.

5) Next, follow the directions on the reflection page by writing down your first thoughts. Does anyone come to mind that you need to interact with? Should you call or visit someone that you love, or someone that you have had or currently have a disagreement with?

6) Finally, write down your intentions to act on these thoughts and feelings, and then *just do it.*

Jesus did not tell His apostles to go and hide after His resurrection. He said to "go and make disciples of all nations". I do not believe that most of us can earn heaven without good works. (Babies and young children are the exceptions). *You cannot **wish** your way into heaven, but you can **work** your way there.*

The Bible should be your GPS (navigation) system to heaven. Use this book as an additional tool to keep you going in the right direction. No matter where you have come from, or what you have been through, there is still time to get on the straight road to your eternal home.

Finally, I'll tell you the same phrase that my high school religion teacher wrote in my senior book: "Stay good and I'll see you in heaven!"

1) ACTIONS

"They profess to know God, but they deny Him by their actions."
Titus 1:16

"I do not understand my own actions. For I do not do what I want, but I do the very thing I hate." Romans 7:15

"For she (wisdom) knows and understands all things, and she will guide me wisely in my actions..." Wisdom 9:11

Thought for today: Do not get down on yourself if you stumble and fall as you progress through this life. Even Jesus fell three times as He walked to Calvary. Get up, as He did, and keep moving forward.

Story 1 - Life Changer

Christ Renews His Parish (CRHP= "Chirp" as it is called), is a Catholic mini-retreat (Saturday-Sunday) held twice per year in many parishes across the country. I attended my first one in the Fall of 2010, and it was a life-changing experience. During the retreat, I realized that though I had faithfully attended Mass on Sundays, Holy Days, and sometimes during the week, that I was only a Catholic spectator, and not a real participant. It was like being a bench warmer on an athletic team, and not ever playing in a real game.

My life changed after that weekend. I now feel that I am truly "off the bench" and really more involved in my church activities. Also, my prayer life has increased, and I am trying to help myself and others to live a more Christian life. I would encourage each of you to attend a CRHP weekend, or any retreat in your faith. A retreat will allow you some special time to search deeply inside your soul for the part of you that is longing to fill a void in your life.

ACTIONS

Your actions will either save you or condemn you.

Your actions tell everyone what you believe, and how strong your faith is.

What can you do today that will be pleasing to God?

Why do you resist God's plan?

Do you know why God created you? Look for your place in history.

God's plan needs you to fulfill your part.

What can you do today that will bring you closer to God?

By your faithful actions, you will be judged.

Put God's plan for your life into action today.

Is there someone who needs your prayers today? Stop and pray for them *right now*.

Prayer: Dear God, let my actions today help as many people as I can.

Topic: **ACTIONS**_____ REFLECTION   Date: _____

Which messages spoke to you on this topic? Underline words or sentences that touched you. Then write down what else came to your mind because of these words:

_____

1. _____

_____

2. _____

_____

3. _____

_____

4. _____

_____

5. _____

_____

Now, write down <u>what you intend to do today or this week</u>, to answer these messages:

_____

1. _____

_____

2. _____

_____

3. _____

_____

4. _____

_____

5. _____

_____

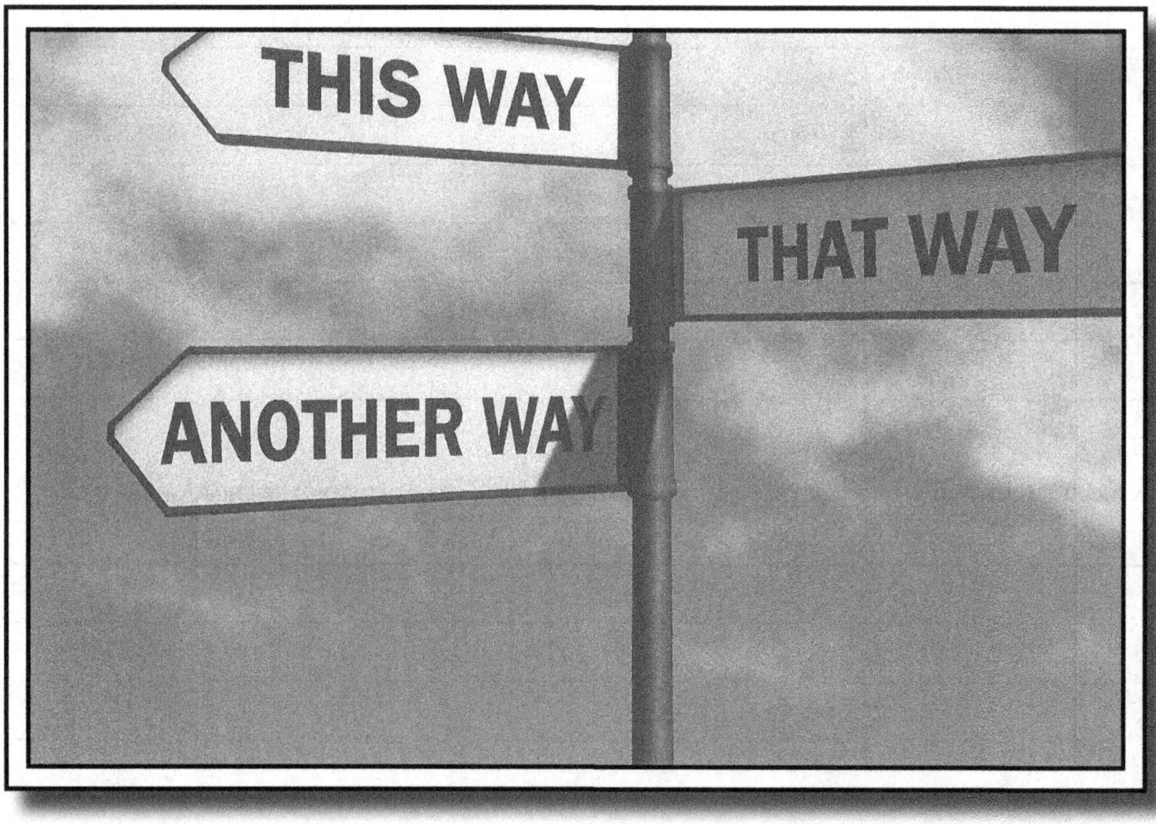
THIS WAY
THAT WAY
ANOTHER WAY

2) CHOICES

"The human mind plans the way, but the Lord directs the steps."
Proverbs 16:9

"Before each person are life and death, and whichever one chooses
will be given." Sirach 15:17

(Jesus said) "You did not choose me but I chose you." John 15:16

Thought for today: Choices are like seeds: the more you plant, the
better chance that the good ones will spring up and grow.

Story 2 - Back To Life

I died once. Well, almost did. I wanted death because I was lost in my self. I pitied the fact that I was in a failing marriage of forty one years, plus I felt increasingly burdened by obligations of taking care of my elderly, melancholic mom. I was lost in a self-absorbed sea of stagnation, an existential morass. No sight of a loving God. I thought I did not need the divine grace and light. I thought that I could control it all. I had no need of this transcendent spirit. So I killed myself. Or I almost did.

My life became unbearable when depression gripped my soul. I wanted relief from all the pain. I forgot that my life was not mine to destroy, but that it belonged to God. I forgot that, as the modern Scottish poet and prophet John Philip Newell writes: I was not just made <u>by</u> God, but that I was made <u>of</u> God. I had been given a divine gift and I was not caring for it.

I did not die. God gave me a second chance. Angels, friends, and family helped me to reclaim that which I had so selfishly rejected. Yes, God gave me one more chance to get it right. I have been given extra credit on my "life loan", and I will use it to live a good and blessed life with God's help.

Now, I wake up every day, take a deep breath, and then I thank and praise God. I am of God. I am alive. I sing the ancient Hebrew song: "Surely it is God who saves me. I will trust in Him and not be afraid."

Carlos A.
Columbia, SC.

CHOICES

Your life history up to today might be bad. Your future could be eternally good. It's up to you.

If God chose to create you, He must have seen something good in you. Now go and find this goodness.

God may not have given you everything that you want, but He has given you all that you need.

If you don't feel good today, ask God for help. If you do feel good today, give Him thanks and praise.

Other people can only guide you. You must help yourself.

God always gives us the right path. It may not always be easy to see, but it is there in front of us. Pray for the wisdom to recognize and the prudence to choose the correct path.

We are all searching for the straightest path to God, although this may not be the easiest path to follow.

Remember, Jesus did not take a luxury jet to heaven. He took the hard path of Calvary and the Cross.

Which road are you on today? Should you stay on this road, or look for another?

Sometimes good people make bad choices. There is still time to turn yourself around. *Start today*!

Prayer: Please God, let me make my future choices in accordance with Your will.

Topic: **CHOICES**_____ REFLECTION   Date: _____

Which messages spoke to you on this topic? Underline words or sentences that touched you. Then write down what else came to your mind because of these words:

_____

1. _____

_____

2. _____

_____

3. _____

_____

4. _____

_____

5. _____

_____

Now, write down <u>what you intend to do today or this week</u>, to answer these messages:

_____

1. _____

_____

2. _____

_____

3. _____

_____

4. _____

_____

5. _____

_____

3) CREATION

"God blessed them, and God said to them: Be fruitful and multiply, and fill the earth and subdue it." Genesis 1:28

"For I am about to create new heavens and a new earth; the former things shall not be remembered or come to mind." Isaiah 65:17

"And He said to them, "Go into all the world and proclaim the good news to the whole creation." Mark 16:15

Thought for today: God did not create each one of us with the same talents. Everyone has different gifts to be used to the best of your ability. Go and use yours wisely.

Story 3 - Relatives Waiting

I was twenty-one in 1969. My father, Claude Smeraglia, was in the last days of his one and one-half year battle with pancreatic cancer. He was in and out of a coma several days before he passed. The last words that I heard him utter were "I'm coming, Tony. I'll be there in a little while."

Up until then, he had been muttering incoherent sounds for a few days. I remember being shocked to hear actual words so clearly spoken by him. His nephew, Tony Smeraglia, has passed some years before. I assume that Tony came to meet Daddy, to take him home.

I have repeated this story often, as I find it comforting to know that just as you don't enter this world alone, nor do you depart this world alone! My dad was a devout Catholic, who felt that the best start for each and every day was attending morning Mass.

C. Chandler

Vestavia, AL.

CREATION

God created you, and that is His gift to you. What you become is your gift to Him.

If a potter can make something beautiful out of mud, clay, and water, just imagine what God can do with you! Let Him mold your life into His new creation. Then celebrate this *new you* and share it with everyone that you meet.

God did not create you to waste any time. He gives some people 90 or 100 years. Others may get only 50 or 60 years. Still others may only get 10 or 20 years. He gives you enough time to do two things: *love Him and your neighbor.* Those two tasks will determine where you will spend eternity.

God doesn't give each of us *equal* time; but He gives each of us *enough* time to fulfill His mission and earn heaven.

What would be the best use of your time this day or this week to accomplish some of His goals for you? Shouldn't you re-arrange your schedule to complete His will?

How much of your weekly schedule involves God? 10%? 5%? 1%? It is a good idea to *tithe your time,* as well as to *tithe your money.*

We all will have to give an accounting someday of how we spent our time, talent, and treasure while here on earth. Make sure that this *heavenly resume* looks good! You only get one "interview" at the end of your life. Make sure that you are ready for it.

Prayer: Dear God, let me become whatever You created me to be, and thereby earn my place in heaven.

Topic: **CREATION**   REFLECTION   Date: _____

Which messages spoke to you on this topic? Underline words or sentences that touched you. Then write down what else came to your mind because of these words:

_____

1. _____

_____

2. _____

_____

3. _____

_____

4. _____

_____

5. _____

_____

Now, write down <u>what you intend to do today or this week</u>, to answer these messages:

_____

1. _____

_____

2. _____

_____

3. _____

_____

4. _____

_____

5. _____

_____

4) FAITH

"And without faith it is impossible to please God, for whoever would approach Him must believe that He exists and that He rewards those who seek Him." Hebrews 11:6

"For just as the body without the spirit is dead, so faith without works is also dead." James 2:26

"Now faith is the assurance of things hoped for, the conviction of things not seen." Hebrews 11:1

Thought for today: "And to the centurion Jesus said, "Go; let it be done for you according to your faith. And (his) servant was healed in that hour." Matthew 8:13

Story 4 - Daily Messages

Since 1981, in a small village in Bosnia (formerly Yugoslavia), named Medjugorje (pronounced Med-ju-gor-ie), the Blessed Virgin Mary has been appearing and giving messages for the world to six people (known as the "visionaries"). Our Lady still appears to some of them every day around 6:50pm, wherever they are.

I visited there in August, 1988, after seeing a story about the visionaries on the news program "20/20". The apparitions originally started in the choir loft at St. James Church in Medjugorje. The six children (at that time) would start saying the Rosary at 6:40pm, and around 6:50pm the children would all drop to their knees as the Blessed Mother would appear to them. At that very moment, the entire church would smell like *fresh roses*. All four hundred people in church could smell the roses, although the wind was not blowing and no roses were planted anywhere around the church.

The Blessed Mother would then give the visionaries a daily message concerning conversion and reconciliation with God. The messages would then be given to the parish priest who would have them printed and given out to all of us the next day.

Also, many persons' rosary chains would turn from *silver to gold* after the apparition. I personally witnessed the smelling of the roses, and saw the rosary chains of many people turn to gold on all eight days that I was there. Faith can move mountains, and your faith can help you get to heaven.

Story 5 - Faith

This is another story about my visit to Medjugorje, Yugoslavia (now Bosnia-see story 4). One night while I was in bed in Medjugorie, I got a knock on the door of my small room at around 11:15pm. As I opened the door, the person outside was excited and said that he had heard that the Blessed Mother might appear on top of the mountain at midnight. (This apparition on the mountaintop had happened to the "visionaries" several times before, always around midnight.)

I jumped up, put on some clothes and headed towards the mountain. Now this was a small farm town with no street lights when I was there in 1988. You had to climb approximately one mile up and around many large rocks to get to the top of the mountain. About six people in my group ran with me to the base of the mountain, but in our haste we had all forgotten our flashlights. The mountain climb was tough during the day, and we had never been there late at night. If someone tried to go back for a flashlight, we would not have been able to get to the top by midnight. We got there and didn't know if we could make it to the top in the dark. However, we looked at the ground and the moon had lit a *perfect path* around the rocks, and we easily made the trip to the top. If you have enough faith, God will give you the guidance that you need.

FAITH

Faith is believing in something that you have not seen or do not fully understand.

When faith increases, fear decreases.

Will you follow Jesus through trials to get to heaven? The Apostles did. Why did they have to suffer and die before they went to heaven? Hadn't they given up everything to follow Jesus? But He asked more of them.

And He will ask for more of you and me. Why? We will understand one day, when our eyes are opened and God's plan is revealed to us. Until then, we must rely on faith. When times get tough, remember the Bible passage: "Blessed are those who have not seen and have believed". (John 20:29)

Faith and love are the greatest gifts that you can receive, but they must be shared.

You are exactly where you need to be at this moment. Believe it!

What are you willing *to do or say today*, in order to inherit eternal life? We should ask ourselves that question weekly or daily, so that we might stay on the right path to God.

Jesus wants us to trust Him and thank Him for everything. He is the Way, the Truth, and the Life. He does not lie and He does not disappoint. He may not give you everything right now, but trust in His knowledge of God's kingdom.

Believe in Him today, that you might live forever with Him in paradise!

Prayer: Jesus, let me share my faith with everyone, so that others may come to know You as I do.

Topic: **FAITH** _____ REFLECTION   Date: _____

Which messages spoke to you on this topic? Underline words or sentences that touched you. Then write down what else came to your mind because of these words:

_____

1. _____

_____

2. _____

_____

3. _____

_____

4. _____

_____

5. _____

_____

Now, write down <u>what you intend to do today or this week</u>, to answer these messages:

_____

1. _____

_____

2. _____

_____

3. _____

_____

4. _____

_____

5. _____

_____

5) GIVING

"Each of you must give as you have made up your mind, not reluctantly or under compulsion, for God loves a cheerful giver." 2 Corinthians 9:7

"And God, who knows the human heart, testified to them by giving them the Holy Spirit, just as He did to us." Acts 15:8

"And whatever you do, in word or deed, do everything in the name of the Lord Jesus, giving thanks to God the Father through Him." Colossians 3:17

Thought for today: Giving is sharing yourself with others, just as Jesus shares Himself with you.

Story 6 - God's Generosity

One morning in the 1978, I was driving to work in Birmingham, Alabama. At a stop light, I noticed a paraplegic man in a small red wagon, pushing his way down the sidewalk. Every move that he made seemed to take all of his strength. Moved to action, I drove around the block until I could find a parking spot. I then got out of my car and went over to his wagon and put down a $50 bill that I had planned on spending for food that week. With tears in his eyes, the man reached over with his bent fingers and quickly pulled the bill under his seat. He smiled and said "God Bless You" to me. Now with tears in *my* eyes, I ran back to my car and went to work.

At that time, I was in a sales job on straight commission. I did not think of the encounter with the paraplegic man again until the end of the day. At that time, I counted up my sales commissions, and I had made exactly $500, a very good day for me in 1978. Then it struck me: God had given me back *exactly ten times* what I had given away that morning!

I only pass on this story to show God's goodness. Now don't expect (as I didn't), that you will be rewarded quickly for what you give away in this life. Actually, it is *better* that your reward should come much later, say as in heaven.

GIVING

You have been given many gifts and blessings in your life. Make sure to share your time, talents, and treasure with others.

Think of someone you know that might be lonely. Make a call or send them a note to let them know that you care about them.

Take someone to lunch that might need you to listen to them. You may find that your problems are small compared to theirs.

Visit a sick or elderly person. You both will benefit!

Be a "problem solver", not a "problem giver".

Don't believe all of the negative news or Internet headlines. The media outlets usually are trying to sell you something, or to challenge your faith.

Help at least *two people* each day, and see how your life will change.

God sees everything, so do good today and you will pile up rewards in heaven!

Prayer: Lord, let me give to others as freely as You give to me.

Topic: **GIVING** _____ REFLECTION   Date: _____

Which messages spoke to you on this topic? Underline words or sentences that touched you. Then write down what else came to your mind because of these words:

_____

1. _____

_____

2. _____

_____

3. _____

_____

4. _____

_____

5. _____

_____

Now, write down <u>what you intend to do today or this week</u>, to answer these messages:

_____

1. _____

_____

2. _____

_____

3. _____

_____

4. _____

_____

5. _____

_____

6) GRACE

"For by grace you have been saved through faith, and this is not your own doing; it is the gift of God…". Ephesians 2:8-9

"But I do not count my life of any value to myself, if only I may finish my course and the ministry that I received from the Lord Jesus, to testify to the good news of God's grace." Acts 20:24

"Those who trust in him will understand truth, and the faithful will abide with him in love, because grace and mercy are upon his holy ones, and he watches over his elect." Wisdom 3:9

Thought for today: Grace will be showered upon those who follow the Heavenly Father's will, and they shall be rewarded forever.

Story 7 - Lasting Memories

I think that I truly felt my faith develop even more when my husband passed away. The morning after he passed, I was being escorted off of the cruise ship. We had been on a week-long cruise when Ernie passed away on the last night of the cruise.

On that Sunday morning as I was being escorted to meet my children who had come to pick me up, a drawing was held for the winner of a gift bag of souvenirs from the ship's gift shop. The name that was drawn was Ernie's. The escort looked at me and said "I am so sorry", and my reply was "that is just Ernie letting me know that he is ok". I remember this as if it were yesterday, and this past April 30th it was 10 years since his passing.

God touched me in so many ways during that time. The fact that my children were together when I had to make that phone call to them. Also, I remember our last wonderful dinner together on the night that he passed.

God has let me know in many ways how my faith has sustained me. He is all-good and helps each of us daily, if we simply will trust in Him.

Jean M.
Pelham, AL.

GRACE

God pours grace on everyone who believes in Him.

God's grace will carry you thru your toughest trials. He never gives you more than you can handle, even though it may seem so at times.

God's grace is a free gift to you. Please share it with others.

God's grace comes from three sources: the Father, the Son, and the Holy Spirit. It also comes from the sacraments, prayers, and good works.

You can't have too much grace. Always beg God for more, so that you may overcome temptations from the world, the flesh, and the devil.

Grace should shine thru you like light thru a window. Keep your window clean, so that His light will shine on all that you meet.

Pray for *grace* and *forgiveness* in the world. These two virtues are desperately needed today!

Take God's grace and follow His will.

Prayer: Holy Spirit, let Your grace fill my heart and soul, so that it may overflow on all that I meet.

Topic: **GRACE**_____ REFLECTION   Date: _____

Which messages spoke to you on this topic? Underline words or sentences that touched you. Then write down what else came to your mind because of these words:

_____

1. _____

_____

2. _____

_____

3. _____

_____

4. _____

_____

5. _____

_____

Now, write down <u>what you intend to do today or this week</u>, to answer these messages:

_____

1. _____

_____

2. _____

_____

3. _____

_____

4. _____

_____

5. _____

_____

7) GUIDANCE

"Where this is no guidance, a nation falls..." Proverbs 11:14

"Make known to me your ways, Lord; teach me your paths. Guide me by your fidelity and teach me, for you are God my Savior..." Psalm 25:4-5

[Prayer for Guidance] "To you, O Lord, I lift up my soul." Psalm 25:1

Thought for today: Faith and the Bible are your navigation (GPS) systems to heaven.

Story 8 ~ My Beliefs

I believe the three most important parts of my Catholic faith are that:

1) Jesus suffered and died on the cross for our sins.
2) Jesus rose from the dead to save us and give us hope.
3) The Mass is celebrated by changing bread and wine into the <u>real</u> body and blood of Jesus for us to receive.

Since I believe all three of the above items, I try to attend daily Mass as often as I can. The real presence of Jesus gives us all hope and the strength to carry on in face of the many difficulties that we encounter each day.

I think that without the Mass and communion, I might be crushed from the weight of all my daily tasks. Just as Simon, the Cyrenian, helped to carry Jesus' cross (Luke 23:26), Jesus helps us to carry our crosses. The real presence of Jesus is with us every day.

Story 9 - The Rosary

The word "rosary" comes from Latin and means a garland of roses, the rose being one of the flowers used to symbolize the Virgin Mary*. *In my personal opinion, the rosary is the most powerful prayer after the saying of the Catholic Mass.* Many Protestants now say the rosary, recognizing it as a truly biblical form of prayer-after all, the prayers that comprise it come mainly from the Bible*. My family has always had a special devotion to the rosary, as I grew up watching my grandmother, grandfather, parents, and many aunts and uncles all saying their daily rosaries.

I believe that many sufferings have been lessened or eliminated, and other requests and prayers answered because of this devotional. I have seen these things happen in my personal life, and have heard about similar help coming to other family members and friends.

You may wish to go to the website, www.catholic.com, and find out more information about this simple but powerful prayer, the rosary.

---

* www.catholic.com/tracts/the-rosary.

GUIDANCE

Pray that the Holy Spirit will guide you where God wants you to go.

You don't have to be perfect today, but you should try to be *good*.

My body is not immortal, but my soul is.

God wants you to do some really small things today, but He wants you to do them *really well*.

No one who follows Jesus will ever be truly lost.

God's path is straight and narrow. Do not stray from it.

Jesus, Mary, and Joseph, guide me to the Father.

Let today be the day that your life changes.

Love of neighbor keeps you on the straight path to heaven.

We were <u>created</u> by the Father, <u>redeemed</u> by the Son, and are <u>guided</u> by the Holy Spirit.

Prayer: Lord God, please keep me on a direct path to you. Let nothing lead me astray. Amen!

Topic: **GUIDANCE** _____ REFLECTION   Date: _____

Which messages spoke to you on this topic? Underline words or sentences that touched you. Then write down what else came to your mind because of these words:

_____

1. _____

_____

2. _____

_____

3. _____

_____

4. _____

_____

5. _____

_____

Now, write down <u>what you intend to do today or this week</u>, to answer these messages:

_____

1. _____

_____

2. _____

_____

3. _____

_____

4. _____

_____

5. _____

_____

8) HAPPINESS

"Take delight in the Lord, and He will give you the desires of your heart." Psalm 37:4

"Be merciful to them, O Master, and keep them safe; bring their lives to fulfillment in happiness and mercy." Tobit 8:17

"Happy is the person who meditates on wisdom and reasons intelligently." Sirach 14:20

Thought for today: You should be happy if you are on your way to heaven. Think about the destination, not the road.

Story 10 - A Spiritual Gift

My Dad was my hero. Last Thanksgiving morning, I went to Mass. After communion, I was sitting praying in the presence of the Lord, and I heard my deceased dad's voice tell me: "I am proud of you". I was overcome with emotion and honestly did not know what to think. I rationalized that I was just being sentimental, because my dad loved Thanksgiving. I did not tell my wife or my mom about this event on that day.

The next evening, my family and I were with my brother Bill's family and the subject of the "afterlife" came up in the discussion. Bill said that he was at also at Mass at St. Jude's on Thanksgiving morning, and for the first time since dad's death seven years ago, he felt his presence. It occurred *at the same time* in Mass as I had heard dad's voice. I ran out of the room in disbelief. This confirmed for me one of the most spiritual gifts that I have received in my life! We never know when the Holy Spirit will speak to us, so we need to be open and listen carefully for God's presence at all times.

I don't think that I would have received or recognized this spiritual gift if I was not making a diligent effort to grow closer to Christ. I still find it difficult to live that way when I am outside of church. Every day presents new challenges, but I can truly tell you that making an effort to be close to Christ has made it easier to do the right thing. I have been working hard to be a better person, a better father, a better husband, a better brother, a better friend, and a better boss.

John A.
Atlanta, GA.

HAPPINESS

You should be happy <u>now</u> because:

God:

    loves you.

    wants you to be happy.

    sent you His only Begotten Son.

    wants to spend eternity with you.

    gave you life. (His choice!)

    sent you a Savior, Jesus.

    is with you now.

    is with you every single day.

    sent Mary to be His and your mother.

    sends the rain, sunshine, flowers, birds, squirrels, sky, wind, seasons, day and night.

    gives you parents, brothers, sisters, relatives, friends, classmates, co-workers and pets.

    gives you food, clothing, shelter, kindness, patience, smiles, tears, and sadness.

    wants you to experience every emotion.

<u>The secret to being happy is not getting everything that you want, but enjoying what you have!</u>

Prayer: Jesus, show me the way to be happy in this life, as I travel towards eternity.

Topic: **HAPPINESS** _____ REFLECTION   Date: _____

Which messages spoke to you on this topic? Underline words or sentences that touched you. Then write down what else came to your mind because of these words:

_____

1. _____

_____

2. _____

_____

3. _____

_____

4. _____

_____

5. _____

_____

Now, write down <u>what you intend to do today or this week</u>, to answer these messages:

_____

1. _____

_____

2. _____

_____

3. _____

_____

4. _____

_____

5. _____

_____

9) HEALING

"Does anyone harbor anger against another, and expect healing from the Lord?" Sirach 28:3

"For the man on whom this sign of healing had been performed was more than forty years old." Acts 4:22

"Rash words are like sword thrusts, but the tongue of the wise brings healing." Proverbs 12:18

Thought for today: Healing your body means to restore it to sound health. This should also apply to your soul.

Story 11 - A Helping Hand

On December 10, 2011, I suffered a major heart attack which required a very rare open heart surgery. So rare in fact, that the University of Maryland Cardiac Center in Baltimore only performs five of these operations per year. I had the septum (the chamber wall inside of the heart), totally rebuilt with tissue from my heart along with the tissue from a cow's heart. I still have an 18-inch scar on my chest where the doctors had to cut me open. I was on the operating table for nearly 13 hours.

During the operation, I felt the presence of someone holding my hand, giving me comfort. It was definitely the hand of a female because it was very soft and petite. I can still feel it today as if the operation was yesterday. At first, I assumed that it was a nurse.

Hours later, the head surgeon and his team came into my intensive care room to introduce himself and to see how I was recovering. I asked the doctor to please thank the nurse who held my hand, because it was greatly appreciated and needed. The doctor looked squarely into my eyes and stated: "Mr. Anthony, no one on my staff was holding your hand; they were all busy trying to save your life." At that moment I knew exactly who had been in that operating room giving me comfort: IT WAS OUR BLESSED MOTHER MARY!

Since then, very few days have gone by that I haven't said my rosary to honor Our Lady. I also thank God daily for giving her to us to love. I can't prove that my visitor was the Blessed Mother or that it wasn't just a dream. But I do know that it happened, and it gave me a sense of security and comfort that everything was going to be fine and that I would survive.

God is good and wonderful. All you have to do is to give Him your trust and He will do the rest.

Charles Anthony
Baltimore, MD.

HEALING

God wants you to be healthy. Do your part (exercise, proper diet, enough sleep, etc.) and then ask for His help.

While you are healing (or waiting to be healed), offer God your sufferings for all of your sins.

Thank God for any healing that comes to you, your relatives or friends. Remember that only one leper, out of ten that were healed, came back to thank Jesus (Luke 18:17). *Be that grateful one*!

Ask for any healing that you want. God can perform miracles. Maybe you will receive one.

Never stop praying for your needs. God hears all prayers, and will answer according to His timetable-not yours.

Your physical healing may not be what you need the most. Also pray for your spiritual healing, which may be more important at this time.

Go to God as a little child, always expecting your request to be answered. God loves a trusting soul!

God can read your mind, but He also wants to hear your words.

Your suffering may be your key to heaven. Even Jesus suffered before rising to the Father.

Help someone that is suffering today. A visit, phone call or card could make their day!

Prayer: Dear God, please bring healing to all that suffer, particularly to (your request).

Topic: **HEALING**_____ REFLECTION   Date: _____

Which messages spoke to you on this topic? Underline words or sentences that touched you. Then write down what else came to your mind because of these words:

_____

1. _____

_____

2. _____

_____

3. _____

_____

4. _____

_____

5. _____

_____

Now, write down <u>what you intend to do today or this week</u>, to answer these messages:

_____

1. _____

_____

2. _____

_____

3. _____

_____

4. _____

_____

5. _____

_____

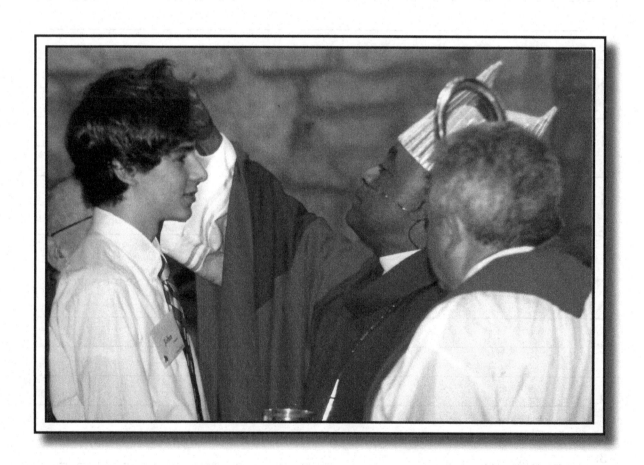

10) HOLINESS

"And may He so strengthen your hearts in holiness that you may be blameless before our God and Father at the coming of our Lord Jesus with all His saints." 1 Thessalonians 3:13

"Your decrees are very sure; holiness befits your house, O Lord, forevermore." Psalm 93:5

"So I will display my greatness and my holiness and make myself known in the eyes of many nations. Then they shall know that I am the Lord." Ezekiel 38:23

Thought for today: Holiness comes from within and touches the people that you meet.

Story 12 ~ My Conversion

In 2001, I had a spiritual awakening while attending Mass at St. Jude's Catholic Church. Over the years, when I attended Mass with my family, I did not go up to receive the Eucharist. I was baptized and confirmed in the Protestant faith and took communion in the various Protestant churches I attended. I knew that this was not acceptable in the Catholic Church and I honored that tradition. I didn't go to Mass with my family every Sunday, but I went a lot. I didn't under-stand the Mass with all the kneeling, standing, sitting, and the rote prayers left me confused. I felt especially *left out* when I couldn't receive communion. My wife and children were members of St. Jude's Church, but I was sitting on the sidelines. Even though I loved the Lord, I couldn't make a commitment. One Sunday, all that changed!

The consecration of the bread and wine had taken place, the Eucharistic ministers were moving to their stations, and the people were beginning to line up to receive the bread and wine. Suddenly, I had a burning desire to go up to the altar. I had an overwhelming feeling that Jesus was personally calling me to come and receive His body and blood. I blurted out to my wife, "I'm going up!"

I received the Eucharist for the first time and my life has never been the same! Later that week, I told Msgr. O'Connor that I wanted to join the Catholic Church. We met at his house for several months and I became an official member of the Church that Easter.

The sacrament of the Eucharist has made a profound impact on my life, on my love for Christ, and His love for me. Now I know what Jesus meant when He said; "it was not you who chose Me, but I who chose you and appointed you to go and bear fruit." I now yearn to go to Mass every Sunday and to receive the body and blood of my Savior, Jesus Christ. When I go to Mass, I talk with Jesus in a private, personal way and I find the peace that only He can give. The music, the ritual, and the closeness with my fellow church members in prayer are great! I thank God and the church for the sacrament of the Eucharist.

Scott McCulley
Atlanta, GA.

Topic: **HOLINESS** _____ REFLECTION   Date: _____

Which messages spoke to you on this topic? Underline words or sentences that touched you. Then write down what else came to your mind because of these words:

_____

1. _____

_____

2. _____

_____

3. _____

_____

4. _____

_____

5. _____

_____

Now, write down <u>what you intend to do today or this week</u>, to answer these messages:

_____

1. _____

_____

2. _____

_____

3. _____

_____

4. _____

_____

5. _____

_____

11) HUMILITY

"The reward for humility and fear of the Lord is riches and honor and life." Proverbs 22:4

"Do nothing from selfish ambition or conceit, but in humility regard others as better than yourselves." Phillipians 2:3

"And all of you must clothe yourselves with humility in your dealings with one another, for God opposes the proud, but gives grace to the humble." 1 Peter 5:5

Thought for today: Don't try to change your friends and family. They are busy trying to change *you*.

Story 13 - St Anthony's Help

In 1999, a six-year old neighbor's son was playing at our house with our two sons. My wife had taken off her wedding ring to wash dishes, and had left it in the kitchen. When the neighbor's son left, she went back looking for her ring, but it was not to be found. We searched the house, just to make sure that she had not moved it to another room. Since we could not find it, she decided to call the neighbor son's mother, just to see if he knew where it was.

The boy then confessed that he had taken the ring, but felt bad about it on the way home. He then threw the ring into a bunch of trees at the back of our yard. There was also a creek that ran by the trees, and seven of us (me, my wife, my two sons, the neighbor's dad and mom, and their son), all searched frantically for about a half an hour all around the trees and creek. In his haste to get rid of it, the boy did not know where he pitched the ring, and we had no real clue where to look.

After combing through the area several times, we gave up and headed back to our houses. My wife was very sad and in tears, so I decided to go back and look just *one more time*. However, I first said a prayer to St. Anthony of Padua, who is the patron saint of lost items. I then went to the street and looked into the trees and saw something shiny on the ground, about 25 feet into the woods. Sure enough, it was my wife's wedding ring! How seven of us missed it is still a mystery to this day, but I like to think that St. Anthony asks God to help us find items that have been lost or misplaced.

St. Anthony is now one of my favorite saints, and I have called upon him hundreds of times to help find lost items over the years. I don't always get immediate help, but I cannot remember a single time where a lost item has not been found, even if it is weeks or months later.

HUMILITY

God must increase. I must decrease.

Humility is realizing that my life is no more important than anyone else's.

Humility means giving your life to God, and asking for salvation in return.

If you want a model of humility, read about Mother Teresa of Calcutta.

I am humble when I realize that God created me for a purpose.

You cannot be humble and impatient at the same time.

You cannot be humble and mean to people at the same time.

If you desire humility, ask the Blessed Mother to show you the way.

Ask God for humility and be happy to show it.

God loves me, warts and all. *Now repeat that.*

Prayer: God, please grant me the courage to be humble today.

Topic: **HUMILITY** _____ REFLECTION   Date: _____

Which messages spoke to you on this topic? Underline words or sentences that touched you. Then write down what else came to your mind because of these words:

_____

1. _____

_____

2. _____

_____

3. _____

_____

4. _____

_____

5. _____

_____

Now, write down <u>what you intend to do today or this week</u>, to answer these messages:

_____

1. _____

_____

2. _____

_____

3. _____

_____

4. _____

_____

5. _____

_____

_____

12) JOY

"Then shall the trees of the forest sing for joy before the Lord, for He comes to judge the earth." 1 Chronicles 16:33

"When they saw that the star had stopped, they were overwhelmed with joy." Matthew 2:10

"Just so, I tell you, there will be more joy in heaven over one sinner who repents than over ninety-nine righteous persons who need no repentance." Luke 15:7

Thought for today: Remember that God does not want His children to be sad. Be joyful and sing His praises!

Story 14 - Healing

Both of my paternal grandparents came over from Italy when they were young. It took about 4 to 6 weeks to come to America by boat in the early 1900s. Because of low medical supplies and contagious diseases, if a child got sick on the boat, the Captain had the right to tell the mother to throw her child overboard to keep the other passengers safe.

My grandmother was six years old when she got sick with a fever one night in 1906 while traveling to America. The Captain stopped by that night and told my great-grandmother that if the child was not well by morning, then she had to drop her in the ocean. Many of my great-grandmother's friends and relatives stayed up and prayed all night to the Blessed Mother for her child to be healed. Well, the next morning the Captain came by and the fever had broken! So God spared my grandmother from being drown in the ocean. <u>It was His choice.</u>

Story 15 - Happy Ending

My grandmother, whom I spoke about in Story 14, was very religious. She was particularly devoted to St. Joseph and the Blessed Mother. She used to sit in a chair by the window in her house and say her rosary every day. She died in 1988, right before her 88th birthday. This story reminds me of her holiness.

My aunt was with my grandmother when she died at their home. Four months after her death, I was at my aunt's house. We were watching a "20/20" news show, and one of the segments was about the reported apparitions of the Blessed Mother to six children (visionaries) in Medjugorje, Yugoslovia (now Bosnia-see story 4).

The news show had one of the children there, and she was asked to describe how the Blessed Mother looked. As the girl (visionary) described her looks and clothing, my aunt burst into tears! We asked my aunt what was wrong and she said that right before her death, my grandmother sat up in bed and said: "look, there is the Blessed Mother!" My aunt thought that she was hallucinating, but asked her to describe what she was seeing.

My grandmother said that the Blessed Mother was so *beautiful,* with dark hair, blue eyes and her clothes were made of gold. This was the <u>exact same description</u> of the Blessed Mother that the young child was giving on "20/20"! I believe that my grandmother lived a holy life, and what a fitting end to have the Blessed Mother come to take her into heaven!

JOY

Joyful are those who know that God is always with them. They overcome trials and evils because their eyes are fixed on heaven.

Today God will answer someone's prayers that you know. Rejoice with them, for your prayers may be answered tomorrow.

If you believe in Jesus and His promises, rejoice that you will one day be in heaven with Him.

Even Jesus suffered and died on Good Friday. But He was raised up on Easter Sunday. So even if you are currently suffering, know that you will be joyful with Him soon.

Be joyful today. Tomorrow is promised to no one.

Don't give up everlasting peace and joy in heaven for a few minutes of pleasure on earth.

Rejoice! Mary is our mother, since we are Jesus' brothers and sisters.

Everyone has a true purpose on earth. Rejoice if you have found yours. Be joyful if you are still searching.

Be joyful to all people that you meet. *Let God's light shine thru you for all to see!*

Prayer: Please God, let my joy help others to come to know You.

Topic: **JOY**_____ REFLECTION   Date: _____

Which messages spoke to you on this topic? Underline words or sentences that touched you. Then write down what else came to your mind because of these words:

_____

1. _____

_____

2. _____

_____

3. _____

_____

4. _____

_____

5. _____

_____

Now, write down <u>what you intend to do today or this week</u>, to answer these messages:

_____

1. _____

_____

2. _____

_____

3. _____

_____

4. _____

_____

5. _____

_____

13) LOVE

"You do well if you really fulfill the royal law according to the scripture, You shall love your neighbor as yourself." James 2:8

"God's love was revealed among us in this way: God sent His only Son into the world so that we might live through Him." 1 John 4:9

"For you love all things that exist, and detest none of the things that you have made..." Wisdom 11:24

Thought for today: Be prepared to love everyone that you meet today. Each one was sent to you by God.

Story 16 ~ True Love

My mom developed early Alzheimer's disease in her 70s, and my dad decided to move them to an assisted living facility in Atlanta, Ga. The property manager suggested that dad live in the more active side of the facility, and not with mom and the other Alzheimer's patients. Dad said no! He told the manager that they had been married for 56 years, and that he would stay in her room, for the reason of that "in sickness and in health" vow that he had taken. So they made an exception for him and let stay on that side. Dad would sit daily after lunch and hold mom's hand until she fell asleep in her wheelchair. He did that for 19 months until she died. The property manager said that she had never seen that kind of love and devotion, and that she now knew the true meaning of marriage.

I believe that is the kind of love that Jesus has for you and me. He will sit by your side and hold onto your hand, no matter what you are called to endure, or how long it takes. That is His true love for you.

Story 17 - Be a Cheerleader

I mentioned that my dad moved to an assisted living facility (see Story 16). He lived there the last 6 years of his life. He loved people, and would get to know as much about you as you would let him. He would then "brag" to others on all that you had accomplished in your life. In fact, a couple of days after he died, the property manager said that "our facility just lost its <u>#1 cheerleader</u> (your dad)".

He also rendered service to the group as long as he could. One of his volunteer jobs was to get up on Sunday morning, take his walker and go knocking door-to-door to wake up the people who wanted to attend the Sunday church service and receive Holy Communion. This goes to show that you can still render God's service at age 88 (and beyond). Hopefully, you and I will still be doing useful tasks until we are called to our future home in heaven.

LOVE

Love is patient, kind, and sharing. *Love means putting the needs of others above your needs.*

St Paul said: "And now faith, hope, and love remain…and the greatest of these is love" (1 Cor. 13:13). Do you believe that?

How can I show my love of God today?

Love is faith in action.

Jesus said to "love your enemies" (Mt 6:44). When have you last done that?

Anger is good if you are angry at the devil. *Love everyone else.*

There is no peace without love.

You can't help everyone. *But you can love them.*

Love is all that matters. Yet it is so often ignored.

You can make a big difference in the world by just loving <u>one</u> extra person today. <u>Try it</u>!

Prayer: Dear God, show me the way to love all people today.

Topic: **LOVE**_____ REFLECTION   Date: _____

Which messages spoke to you on this topic? Underline words or sentences that touched you. Then write down what else came to your mind because of these words:

_____

1. _____

_____

2. _____

_____

3. _____

_____

4. _____

_____

5. _____

_____

Now, write down <u>what you intend to do today or this week</u>, to answer these messages:

_____

1. _____

_____

2. _____

_____

3. _____

_____

4. _____

_____

5. _____

_____

_____

St. Bernadette of Lourdes

Virgin, Incorruptible
Ex capillis (a hair)

Also known as:
Bernadette Soubirous; the
Sleeping Saint of Nevers.

Feast:
16 April.

Profile:

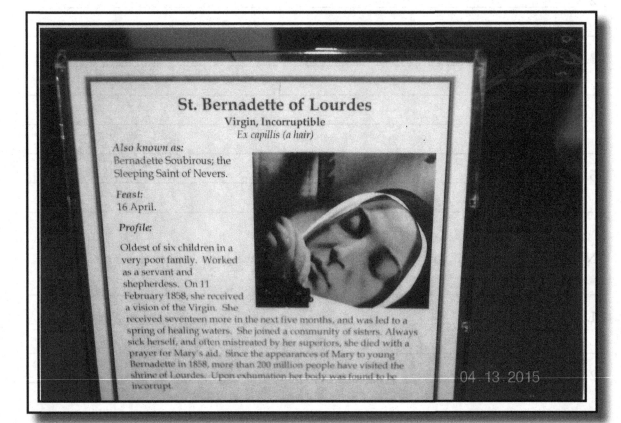

Oldest of six children in a
very poor family. Worked
as a servant and
shepherdess. On 11
February 1858, she received
a vision of the Virgin. She
received seventeen more in the next five months, and was led to a
spring of healing waters. She joined a community of sisters. Always
sick herself, and often mistreated by her superiors, she died with a
prayer for Mary's aid. Since the appearances of Mary to young
Bernadette in 1858, more than 200 million people have visited the
shrine of Lourdes. Upon exhumation her body was found to be
incorrupt.

14) PAIN AND SUFFERING

"He will wipe every tear from their eyes. Death will be no more; mourning and crying and pain will be no more, for the first things have passed away." Revelation 21:4

"For just as the sufferings of Christ are abundant for us, so also our consolation is abundant through Christ." 2 Corinthians 1:5

"I consider that the sufferings of this present time are not worth comparing with the glory about to be revealed to us." Romans 8:18

Thought for today: From time to time, ask God to take suffering from someone that you know, and give it to you. You both will be helped.

Story 18 - A True Miracle

It was the last high school game week for football during our senior season. Who better to be standing behind than a large lineman (also State discus & shot put champ), while we tried to bounce rocks off the bleachers. I had my helmet on but the next thing I knew something hit my left eye as well as my helmet, sounding like a gunshot!

My knees buckled and I hit the ground thinking someone driving by John Carroll Field had just shot me! Coach Porter was the first to get to me and he tried to look at my eye. However, all I saw was extremely painful sunlight.

Fortunately, one of our team members (whose father was an eye doctor), had gone into the coach's office and called his dad. His order was to get me to the hospital as soon as possible, so they did.

Long story short, I was blind in my left eye from a rock hitting it. Lacerated lens and blood vessels internally ruptured. Both eyes had to be bandaged so that I could not move my eyes. By the end of the week, the eye doctor said if the internal bleeding started again, they would have to operate with a good chance that I would lose my eye. Having my classmates visiting was great but visitation was cut short, because the doctor did not want me talking or moving my head in any way.

On Friday, right after the football team visited, my youngest brother, thinking that I needed a little "humor" in my situation, tried to prank me. It worked but I could also feel the blood leaking inside my eye…looks like I would lose it.

Sunday, our parish priest came by and asked if I minded if he anointed my bandaged eye with water from the fountain of Lourdes, France. He had been saving it for a special time and need. I asked the last person that came into my room that night, to explain the story of Lourdes, which is where the Blessed Mother had appeared to St. Bernadette[*]. I then thought that if angels had touched the water, it had to be better than the medicine that I was taking and not working.

The next morning, the doctor came in for the big unveiling. If the eye was still bleeding, then he would cut it out. The doctor noticed that I was following him around the room with my eyes. He was shocked and said, "you can see me?"….YES!!!

---

[*] See "Lourdes Apparitions" at Wikipedia.org

I never got the bad cataract (its growth stopped that day), nor glaucoma, nor any of the other problems that they said I would get. The Lourdes water had worked. After all, God does not perform partial miracles!

Mike N.
Orlando, FL.

PAIN AND SUFFERING

If you are suffering today, just look at Jesus on the cross. <u>Your pain is small compared to His</u>.

Pain is watching a loved one suffer. It hurts more than if it were your own pain, since you feel powerless to give them immediate help.

You may not be able to help someone physically or financially; but you can pray to the One that can (God).

You were not born into heaven, but it is possible to get there from here.

If you love God, you can ask Him to take away your pain. Our loving Father always hears His children.

The pain of the cross was forgotten on the third day, when Jesus rose from the dead. So too, will it be with your life. Your sufferings will be nothing compared to the joy of seeing God!

Your <u>pain</u> might be your <u>train</u> to heaven.

Why do I need God? Because He has given me everything that is good.

You cannot understand your life and sufferings because your mind is not fully enlightened. One day it will all be clear. *That day is coming soon.*

Prayer: Dear Jesus, thank You for letting me share some of your pain and suffering. May it lead me to eternal happiness with You.

Topic: **PAIN & SUFFERING** _____ REFLECTION Date: _____

Which messages spoke to you on this topic? Underline words or sentences that touched you. Then write down what else came to your mind because of these words:

_____

1. _____

_____

2. _____

_____

3. _____

_____

4. _____

_____

5. _____

_____

Now, write down <u>what you intend to do today or this week</u>, to answer these messages:

_____

1. _____

_____

2. _____

_____

3. _____

_____

4. _____

_____

5. _____

_____

15) PATIENCE

"Be patient, therefore, beloved, until the coming of the Lord."
James 5:7

"But for that very reason I received mercy, so that in me…Jesus Christ might display the utmost patience, making me an example to those who would come to believe in Him for eternal life." 1 Timothy 1:16

"Do not put us to shame, but deal with us in your patience and in your abundant mercy." Daniel 3:42

Thought for today: If teachers had no patience, then very few of us would ever learn anything.

Story 19 - A Watchful Eye

My mother and I were coming home going south on I-65 from Huntsville to Birmingham, Alabama. I was driving. About the time we got to Cullman, which is nearly halfway home, I started getting sleepy and began dozing. My foot automatically relaxed. My mother, who didn't know that I was falling asleep, asked why I had slowed down so much.

About two minutes in front of us, there was a 3 or 4-car pileup. When we got there, the traffic had not even started to back up. If I had not gotten sleepy and slowed down, we would have been right in the middle of this accident.

I know that God, Jesus, and the Blessed Mother were all in that car with us. The simple fact that I kept the car in the road and slowed down just in time, meant that we were being protected. I have always had a strong faith, but this is one event that I think about all the time and thank God for watching over me. It has been over ten years since this incident happened.

J.B.
Birmingham, AL.

PATIENCE

Patience attracts peace.

Patience is listening to a child speak, no matter how long it takes them to tell their story.

Patience is hearing an older person tell a story that you have heard many times before, and listening to them repeat all of the details that they can remember.

Patience is hearing a friend or loved one tell you their troubles, while you quietly wait to tell yours.

Patience is being slow to anger, but quick to forgive someone.

<u>Are you patiently waiting for heaven, or speeding in another direction?</u>

Be thankful that God is patient with you. He knows the special talents that you have, and how He wants you to use them.

Pray that you will have patience with others. Remember the parable of the Master that forgave a large debt to his servant. But also remember what happened when that same servant was not patient with *his* debtor. (Mt 18: 23-35)

Prayer: Father, wait patiently for me. Let me do Your will always.

Topic: **PATIENCE** _____ REFLECTION   Date: _____

Which messages spoke to you on this topic? Underline words or sentences that touched you. Then write down what else came to your mind because of these words:

_____

1. _____

_____

2. _____

_____

3. _____

_____

4. _____

_____

5. _____

_____

Now, write down <u>what you intend to do today or this week</u>, to answer these messages:

_____

1. _____

_____

2. _____

_____

3. _____

_____

4. _____

_____

5. _____

_____

_____

16) PEACE

"Jesus said to them again, Peace be with you. As the Father has sent me, so I send you." John 20:21

"Blessed are the peacemakers, for they will be called children of God." Matthew 5:9

"I have said this to you, so that in Me you may have peace. In the world you face persecution. But take courage; I have conquered the world!" John 16:33

Thought for today: You cannot force peace with anyone. Simply offer it to them and see what happens.

Story 20 ~ The Cardinal

My wife's father had cancer in 2009. Since her mother died suddenly a few years earlier, my father-in-law said that after he died, he would try to send my wife a sign that he was OK. He later died in October of 2009.

In December of 2009, we were in Huntsville, Alabama at my father-in-law's home where he had died. My wife and her sister were standing in the driveway talking to each other, and no one else was around them. Suddenly, a golf ball came rolling out of the garage, and stopped close to them. (Their dad had been an avid golfer in his life, and very much a practical joker). Since no one was in the garage, my wife and her sister both said that it must be a sign that their dad was OK.

A couple of weeks later, still in December, my wife was feeling sad at home, since it was going to be her first Christmas without her dad. One morning she looked out the kitchen window and a cardinal flew to the bird feeder that we had outside the window on the porch. The cardinal turned around and stared at both of us, and then flew towards us and landed on the window sill. He (it was a bright red male cardinal), then flew to the tree in the back of the yard. He came to that tree every day until after Christmas.

My wife and I are convinced that it was a sign that her dad was alright. Whenever we felt sad thinking about her dad, the cardinal would fly onto the porch and stare at us. We have since bought many items with a cardinal on it, and yes, the cardinal still comes around to see us often.

PEACE

Peace can only come from God. You cannot create it by yourself.

Try to promote peace in your family first. Then work for it with your friends, community, and all that you meet.

Pray today for peace in the world. This need has never been greater.

God grants peace to those who *trust* in Him.

Jesus said "Peace be with you." (Luke 24:36). Why are your fighting it?

Ask for peace with your enemies. It will shock, surprise, and disarm them.

The greatest treasure that you can find on earth is internal peace.

If someone has died before you made peace with them, then pray for them now. You can still obtain peace for yourself.

Your children/parents/siblings want peace with you, but don't know how to ask for it. Help them!

Take one day per week and pray for peace. *Watch how the world and you will change*!

Prayer: Father, let me become a "peacemaker" to all that I meet.

Topic: **PEACE**_____ REFLECTION   Date: _____

Which messages spoke to you on this topic? Underline words or sentences that touched you. Then write down what else came to your mind because of these words:

_____

1. _____

_____

2. _____

_____

3. _____

_____

4. _____

_____

5. _____

_____

Now, write down <u>what you intend to do today or this week</u>, to answer these messages:

_____

1. _____

_____

2. _____

_____

3. _____

_____

4. _____

_____

5. _____

_____

17) PRAYER

"Hear my prayer, O God; give ear to the words of my mouth." Psalm 54:2

"Regard your servant's prayer and his plea, O Lord my God, heeding the cry and the prayer that your servant prays to you today…" 1 Kings 8:28

"So I tell you, whatever you ask for in prayer, believe that you have received it, and it will be yours." Mark 11:24

Thought for today: Pray that you will accept and follow God's plan for you.

Story 21 - A Burning Answer

My husband Pat was finishing up school at Tennessee Temple University, getting his Master of Divinity degree in Theology. Pat is a chaplain for Hospice, and has been in Ministry for about 40 years.

It was the Spring of 1988. We lived in Chattanooga, Tennessee while he was in school, but we wanted to live in nearby Catoosa County in Georgia, a family community with a good school system. We signed our children up to play ball that Spring, and began the process of looking at houses. We looked everywhere, following leads from realtors, family, and friends. However, we soon became discouraged.

One afternoon, after looking most of the day, we decided to pull off the road to pray. We asked God if He was in favor of this move. If He wasn't, then to please guide us in another direction. We prayed: God we need a "burning bush experience!" The "burning bush" is a scripture reference in Exodus 3:1-4, that tells about God speaking to Moses out of a burning bush. Through this remarkable event, God speaks to Moses in an undeniable way. That's what we needed: to know that God was in our lives and in favor of this move.

We prayed and continued on the country road that we had been traveling. We then came to a house that was for sale. It looked nice, and possibly in our price range, so we took the house number down. We did not know the name of the road, and continued a mile or so to the end of it. Finally, we came to the street marker and we wrote down in amazement the name of the road..."Burning Bush"! We made an offer on the house and everything went sailing through. God was indeed in this move, and almost 30 years later we are still in this house after raising three children, attending church, teaching (I am a teacher), and ministering in this community.

God has certainly guided our steps over the years in so many ways. We have had to "step out in faith" trusting the unseen, but standing on His Word and promises more than a few times. But that day will be forever etched in our memories: the day God revealed Himself to us in an undeniable way.

Grace A. Davis
Ringgold, GA.

PRAYER

Praying is asking or thanking God for His help.

Your prayers are always heard by God, although not always answered as you wish.

Your soul needs prayer as your body needs food.

Pray for your children. God wants you to bring them to heaven to meet His family.

Pray for your enemies. This action will help both of you.

Praying is caring. Caring is love. God is love.

If this was your last day on earth, what would you pray for?

Start each day with a prayer of thanksgiving. The rest of the day will take care of itself.

I believe that the best Catholic prayer, after the Mass, is the rosary.

God doesn't *need* your prayers, but He wants to *hear* them.

Pray for the unborn. Their life depends on their *mother's choice.*

Prayer: Jesus, please let me pray to the Father as you did.

Topic: **PRAYER**_____ REFLECTION   Date:_____

Which messages spoke to you on this topic? Underline words or sentences that touched you. Then write down what else came to your mind because of these words:

_____

1. _____

_____

2. _____

_____

3. _____

_____

4. _____

_____

5. _____

_____

Now, write down <u>what you intend to do today or this week</u>, to answer these messages:

_____

1. _____

_____

2. _____

_____

3. _____

_____

4. _____

_____

5. _____

_____

18) PRESENCE OF JESUS

"Then He took a loaf of bread, and when He had given thanks, He broke it and gave it to them, saying, This is My Body, which is given for you. Do this in remembrance of Me." Luke 22:19

"And He did the same with the cup after supper, saying, This cup that is poured out for you is the new covenant in my blood." Luke 22:20

"Jesus said to them, I am the bread of life. Whoever comes to me will never be hungry, and whoever believes in me will never be thirsty." John 6:35

Thought for today: Jesus is always present in the world. Talk to Him frequently, for He always hears you.

Story 22 - Body of Christ

John 6:51

I am the living bread that came down from heaven; whoever eats this bread will live forever; and the bread that I will give is my flesh, for the life of the world.

I attended Marist Catholic High School in Atlanta, Ga. During one of the Wednesday morning Masses in the Marist chapel, I can still remember exactly where I was sitting. I came back from communion, sat down and was praying.

I was then hit with a revelation. It was like something came over me, possessed my thoughts, made me completely and undoubtedly aware and conscious that I had just received the Body of Christ.

This was no symbol, no likeness, no religious token to be taken lightly; it was the real deal. The God who humbled himself to become man and was crucified for my sins was REAL, AND I had just partaken in Him through the Holy Eucharist!

THE ACTUAL Body-of-Christ was sitting there on my tongue.

Matthew 28:20

And behold, I am with you always, until the end of the age.

I was not having any doubts about my faith, but from that moment on I knew without any hesitation that what I professed to believe in as a Catholic was real, and that I was being cared for and noticed by God. I still go back to this moment when God seems far away, when things are crumbling around me, when life is hard and the world seems unforgivably rotten.

Barry S.
Atlanta, GA.

THE PRESENCE OF JESUS

Jesus is with you 24 hours per day, seven days per week. His love has no beginning and no end.

Jesus wants to give you His peace, but you must put aside your daily cares and ask for it.

Tomorrow's problems cannot come now, so relax and give yourself to Jesus fully. This action will help you fulfill God's will today.

If you concentrate on the presence of Jesus, your worries and anxieties will melt away.

Jesus is present to guide your day and your actions. Look for Him in each person and situation that you encounter.

Jesus wants you to realize that your fears and problems are small compared to His love and peace.

Jesus still loves you, even when you feel unlovable.

Jesus wants you to <u>trust</u> and <u>thank</u> Him constantly for all that you have been given.

Jesus said that He would never leave us. "And behold, I am with you always, until the end of the age". (Mt 28:20)

Prayer: Jesus, thank you for Your everlasting Presence. Please speak to me daily.

Topic: **THE PRESENCE OF JESUS** REFLECTION   Date: _____

Which messages spoke to you on this topic? Underline words or sentences that touched you. Then write down what else came to your mind because of these words:

_____

1. _____

_____

2. _____

_____

3. _____

_____

4. _____

_____

5. _____

_____

Now, write down <u>what you intend to do today or this week</u>, to answer these messages:

_____

1. _____

_____

2. _____

_____

3. _____

_____

4. _____

_____

5. _____

_____

_____

19) RECONCILIATION/ CONFESSION

"If we confess our sins, He who is faithful and just will forgive us our sins and cleanse us from all unrighteousness." 1 John 1:9

"I will give you the keys of the kingdom of heaven, and whatever you bind on earth will be bound in heaven, and whatever you loose on earth will be loosed in heaven." Matthew 16:19

"All the prophets testify about Him that everyone who believes in Him receives forgiveness of sins through His name." Acts 10:43

Thought for today: Reconciling with God makes you feel born again.

Story 23 - Spiritual Renewal

Last Spring, at the Christ Renews His Parish retreat, I experienced a renewal that has changed my life. Prior to the retreat, I was mesmerized by a lyric in the Bruce Springsteen song, *Rocky Ground*. The lyric describes Christ as He clears out the Temple, restoring order, and upsetting the money changers' tables. That lyric also urges the shepherd to find his scattered flock and move them to higher ground.

These messages resonated with me throughout the retreat, mentally and emotionally communicating to me that I am responsible for the salvation of my wife and children. In this world of darkness, God has appointed me to be the shepherd of my family. He has entrusted me with protecting them. He has placed their spiritual growth into my hands, to lead my wife and children to "higher ground".

Since my renewal, I have been more inspired to spend time in prayer; to set aside time daily to listen to God in quiet contemplation; and to attend a morning bible study with my fellow brothers. Now, through God's grace, I have been given a new perspective, or what I call a "new set of glasses" to read the Scripture through.

I believe that with God all things are possible, and that each Christian can impact the kingdom of God. However, the change must begin with me and my heart. I must be "all-in" for God and love those around me, starting with my amazing wife and children, and then to the greater community.

John T.
Atlanta, GA

RECONCILIATION / CONFESSION

Confessing your sins is like taking a shower. The more often you do it, the cleaner you feel.

A good confession is not just about asking forgiveness for past sins, but about trying to sin no more in the future.

The priest doesn't forgive your sins by himself. God forgives your sins through the priest.

An examination of conscience before confession should make you realize when and how often you are sinning. It should also help you to break your "habits of sin".

Confession before receiving the Eucharist is like washing your hands before a meal.

God doesn't expect you to be perfect; but He expects you to try.

<u>Be glad that God doesn't hold any grudges.</u>

You don't have to go to church this Sunday, but you should.

God will forgive your sins, but *you must try to give them up.*

Prayer: Lord, let me confess my sins often, so that I can receive Your grace through the Holy Spirit.

RECONCILIATION /

Topic: **CONFESSION** _____ REFLECTION   Date: _____

Which messages spoke to you on this topic? Underline words or sentences that touched you. Then write down what else came to your mind because of these words:

_____

1. _____

_____

2. _____

_____

3. _____

_____

4. _____

_____

5. _____

_____

Now, write down <u>what you intend to do today or this week</u>, to answer these messages:

_____

1. _____

_____

2. _____

_____

3. _____

_____

4. _____

_____

5. _____

_____

20) SACRIFICE

"...let yourselves be built into a spiritual house, to be a holy priesthood, to offer spiritual sacrifices acceptable to God through Jesus Christ." 1 Peter 2:5

"Offer right sacrifices, and put your trust in the Lord." Psalm 4:5

"Gather to me my faithful ones, who made a covenant with me by sacrifice." Psalm 50:5

Thought for today: God never asks for more than you can give.

Story 24 ~ A Father's Memory

My father passed away July 29, 1986, ten short months after his initial diagnosis of melanoma cancer. He was 52 years old. I was 22. He was surrounded by three of his six children. We prayed the rosary, and my mom rocked my dad in her arms as he breathed his last. It was an awesome death, and I could sense the soul of my father departing to go meet Jesus. We sent him home in a blaze of glory.

I remember the funeral Mass, and how proud that I was to see the church packed. I remember at the sign of peace hugging my brother David and crying for a very long time. We simply couldn't let go of each other.

I remember at the grave site, as we were departing, my mom rapped her wedding ring on the wooden casket, and said through her tears, "Not my will, but yours be done." I thought of the words of Simeon to the Blessed Mother: "A sword shall pierce your heart." My mom is my hero, my rock of faith.

My father's death was an incredible sacrifice. My dad never complained, never asked "Why me"? He took it like a man. His death allowed me to have strong relationships with all my brothers and sisters. His death bonded us as a family in a very mystical way. All six of us have solid marriages and no divorces. All of us are practicing Catholics. I believe that this is no coincidence. Also, I know that dad would have gotten a kick out of his 17 grandkids.

Man, how I miss my dad! I will never get over it. I have instead just learned to hold onto these memories. His death has helped me to embrace my own fatherhood, to realize how short our lives are, and to enjoy every moment with my wife and sons.

Paul Y.
Sandy Springs, GA.

SACRIFICE

What can you offer God today, in thanksgiving for your many blessings?

My sacrifices are tiny, when I look at Jesus' sacrifice on the cross.

What sacrifice from me, would make God happy today?

Give everything to God, and He will give you everything that you need.

God asks that you come to know, love, and serve Him thru others. It is a simple request, but sometimes hard to do.

Find a person in need today and help them. It is one of the reasons that you were born.

Everyone wants some of your time – even God.

What sacrifices would you make today, if this was your last day on earth?

No sacrifice will go unrewarded. However, it is better to be rewarded later (*in heaven*) rather than sooner (*on earth*).

Prayer: Heavenly Father, thank you for the sacrifice of Your Son, who has redeemed us.

Topic: **SACRIFICE** _____ REFLECTION   Date: _____

Which messages spoke to you on this topic? Underline words or sentences that touched you. Then write down what else came to your mind because of these words:

_____

1. _____

_____

2. _____

_____

3. _____

_____

4. _____

_____

5. _____

_____

Now, write down <u>what you intend to do today or this week</u>, to answer these messages:

_____

1. _____

_____

2. _____

_____

3. _____

_____

4. _____

_____

5. _____

_____

21) SERVICE

"Render service with enthusiasm, as to the Lord and not to men and women, knowing that whatever good we do, we will receive the same again from the Lord..." Ephesians 6:7

"I am grateful to Christ Jesus our Lord, who has strengthened me, because he judged me faithful and appointed me to His service." 1 Timothy 1:12

"I know your works-your love, faith, service, and patient endurance. I know that your last works are greater than the first." Revelation 2:19

Thought for today: One day you will have to render an accounting for your service to others.

Story 25 - St. Therese of Lisieux

In April, 2015, a traveling "Treasures of the Church" exhibit came to our church in Atlanta. "Treasures" is a ministry of evangelization of the Catholic Church. Run by Fr. Carlos Martins of the *Companions of the Cross*, its purpose is to give people an experience of the living God through an encounter with the relics of His saints in the form of exposition."* After a presentation by Fr. Martins, those in attendance have an opportunity to hold and venerate the relics of some of their favorite saints.

Fr. Martins said that you could pick up the relics and some people may feel a "hot or cold" sensation, which might mean that this could be a special saint for you.

As we were touching and picking up the enclosed relics, my wife said that the one of St. Therese of Lisieux felt hot to her. I then touched it, but it did not feel hot to me. We then went home that Monday night having been very impressed with the presentation and the relics.

My wife had been suffering with vertigo for the past week, which makes you very dizzy. She had prayed to St. Therese on Monday night, without telling me. However, on Wednesday morning, she woke up to tell me that her vertigo was gone! She has no doubt that her prayers were answered by St. Therese's intercession. My wife now has a special devotion to a new Saint that she had not previously studied.

Catholics do not pray to be cured by saints, but to be <u>cured by God</u> through the intercession of the saint. Normally, to become a modern day saint (non-martyred) in the Catholic Church, a requirement of at least two miracles must be attributed and authenticated to that saint." Do not doubt God's ability to use saints to help you. He will explain everything to you, once you get to heaven!

---

* For more information, see: <u>www.treasuresofthechurch.com</u>
** Per: <u>catholicdoors.com/faq/qu221.htm</u>

SERVICE

Whom can you serve today?

Dear Jesus, let my life follow the Father's will by serving my brothers and sisters.

Today, I will be a servant to all those that I meet.

God is sending you someone that needs your help today. Please look for that person.

<u>You can always help someone, if only to pray for them.</u>

May my life be pleasing to God, the Creator who sent me.

Share what you have with your brothers and sisters. It is part of your purpose in life.

Jesus said: "I am among you as the one who serves" (Luke 22:27). We should imitate Him.

God is taking notes: *What have you done for His kingdom today?*

Prayer: Dear God, let my service to others today be according to Your heavenly will.

Topic: **SERVICE** _____ REFLECTION   Date: _____

Which messages spoke to you on this topic? Underline words or sentences that touched you. Then write down what else came to your mind because of these words:

_____

1. _____

_____

2. _____

_____

3. _____

_____

4. _____

_____

5. _____

_____

Now, write down <u>what you intend to do today or this week</u>, to answer these messages:

_____

1. _____

_____

2. _____

_____

3. _____

_____

4. _____

_____

5. _____

_____

22) SIMPLICITY

"...Jesus said, Let the little children come to me, and do not stop them; for it is to such as these that the kingdom of heaven belongs." Matthew 19:14

"O simple ones, learn prudence; acquire intelligence, you who lack it." Proverbs 8:5

"The law of the Lord is perfect, reviving the soul; the decrees of the Lord are sure, making wise the simple..." Psalm 19:7

Thought for today: God did not create everyone to do something big. But He did create everyone to do <u>something</u>.

Story 26 ~ Peaceful Passing

Around 2001, one of my younger sisters, Monica, developed brain cancer. Monica was the fourth of five children, and mom and dad's special child. While Monica was just a little slower than the rest of us, she was fully functioning and graduated from high school. As Monica never married, she lived in an upstairs apartment with my mother after dad died. Needless to say, they were very close.

My mom had retired as the Chief night nurse at St. Joseph's Hospital in Savannah, Ga., and she wasn't called "the general" for nothing. Her sisters were also registered nurses, and so were some of mom's friends. She set up *24-hour nursing shifts* for all of her sisters to help. Even though mom took charge and brought in a hospital bed in place of the dining room table, Monica's cancer still progressed.

It was a moment of grace for me to watch my little sister so peacefully give herself up to the Lord. Knowing that she was dying, when she was asked how she was feeling, she would just smile and say: "it's up to the big man upstairs".

One morning at 9am, while mom and I were holding her hands and saying a rosary, Monica took her last breath. It was the most peaceful thing that I had ever seen. I could just feel God reaching down and touching my mother's heart, as Monica's soul was being lifted up to heaven.

John Rowland
Sandy Springs, GA.

SIMPLICITY

God loves simple people.

Simple can mean trusting and thankful.

God's plan is simple: love one another.

Do small simple acts with a large amount of love.

Accomplish what you can in this life. If you can do something big – do it! If you can do something small – do it! God knows what you are capable of.

Simply pray for forgiveness and healing. These are not small things.

Do not worry about yourself today. Help someone who has bigger problems.

Your talents are seeds. Be sure to plant them regularly.

Pray for the elderly and sick. You might need <u>their</u> prayers soon.

<u>Do you live your "Sunday Faith" on the other six days?</u>

I am not yet who **I** want to be, but I am striving to be the person that **God** wants me to be.

Prayer: Dear Jesus, You love simple people. Let me become one of them.

Topic: **SIMPLICITY** _____ REFLECTION   Date: _____

Which messages spoke to you on this topic? Underline words or sentences that touched you. Then write down what else came to your mind because of these words:

_____

1. _____

_____

2. _____

_____

3. _____

_____

4. _____

_____

5. _____

_____

Now, write down <u>what you intend to do today or this week</u>, to answer these messages:

_____

1. _____

_____

2. _____

_____

3. _____

_____

4. _____

_____

5. _____

_____

23) TEMPTATION

"Blessed is anyone who endures temptation. Such a one has stood the test and will receive the crown of life that the Lord has promised to those who love Him." James 1:12

"No testing has overtaken you that is not common to everyone. God is faithful, and He will not let you be tested beyond your strength…" 1 Corinthians 10:13

"But those who want to be rich fall into temptation and are trapped by many senseless and harmful desires…" 1 Timothy 6:9

Thought for today: You will be tempted until the day that you die, so be prepared to fight these temptations every day.

Story 27 - Protection from Above

It was a beautiful sunny afternoon. We had been in our new neighborhood only nine months. My three daughters and two of the neighborhood children had been throwing acorns from our oak tree at each other in our front yard, while I was sitting in my fold-up sports chair, as I was very pregnant with our son.

The next door neighbors owned a painting company and their new employee had come outside impeccably groomed, clean shaven with a handlebar mustache, a fresh haircut, and a clean smell of cologne or after shave. His white pants and white shirt were starched and professionally pressed. When I spoke with him, his manner of speech was flawless, enunciating every syllable and using vocabulary above his employment. He began by mimicking the kids and throwing acorns with them. Within a few short minutes, Mother Nature had called me and I stood up excusing myself, and asked if the gentleman could "just look after the kids for a few minutes?"

Instead of making my normal 180-degree turn and taking only five or six steps across my lawn to enter my front door, I started walking down my own paved driveway. I stopped abruptly as I thought it was silly of me to hear a voice asking a strange question when I reached the end. However, I kept walking. The voice grew much louder and repeated the same question: "Why is he playing on their level"? I glanced backward. Everyone, including the gentleman, was throwing acorns at each other. "Yes," I thought, "Why was a grown man throwing acorns with children?"

I then articulated to the gentleman, making sure he followed my new directions, to please make sure that both he and the kids walked inside the neighbor's house. I gently shouted to my daughters to follow me inside our house. I never saw the gentleman again.

Approximately two months later, my doorbell rang in the early afternoon, and before my usual perfunctory greeting of hello, the two well-dressed gentlemen both showed me their badges. They were FBI agents. They handed me with a picture of a handlebar-mustached gentleman. "Yes, I did recognize him," I said. Their next question directed at me was, "Did he have any contact with your children?" "No!" The agents then informed me, "He is a child molester." The FBI arrested the pedophile the day after they had spoken to me.

Two days later, I reiterated to my next door neighbor about hearing that voice and that question. We thanked OUR HEAVENLY FATHER, for making me listen to HIS question: "Why is he playing on their level?" It was GOD who protected our children on that day!

D.M.P.

(City and State withheld on request)

TEMPTATION

Everyone is tempted to sin and evil. Even Jesus was tempted in the desert. "When the devil had finished every temptation, he departed from Him for a time." (Luke 4:13). Since this bible passage states that the devil left Him (Jesus) "for a time", we can assume that the devil came back to tempt Jesus again.

What is your greatest temptation? How can you fight it?

Pray often and ask God to help in the battle for your eternal soul.

The <u>devil</u> wants you to think that there is no hell, so that you might spend eternity with him.

The <u>world</u> wants you to think that there is no heaven, so that you might do anything that you want here.

The <u>flesh</u> tells you "if it feels good, then do it", even though you might hurt God and others by your actions.

<u>Remember, no matter how much evil is in the world, Jesus has and will conquer it</u>!

God gave you free will. What will you give Him in return?

Today and every day, you must choose between "good" and "evil". *What is your choice?*

Prayer: Dear Lord, I long to see Your face. Please send angels to fight for my soul.

Topic: **TEMPTATION** _____ REFLECTION   Date: _____

Which messages spoke to you on this topic? Underline words or sentences that touched you. Then write down what else came to your mind because of these words:

_____

1. _____

_____

2. _____

_____

3. _____

_____

4. _____

_____

5. _____

_____

Now, write down <u>what you intend to do today or this week</u>, to answer these messages:

_____

1. _____

_____

2. _____

_____

3. _____

_____

4. _____

_____

5. _____

_____

24) THANKSGIVING

"Enter His gates with thanksgiving, and his courts with praise. Give thanks to Him, bless His name." Psalm 100:4

"Blessed be the God and Father of our Lord Jesus Christ, the Father of mercies and the God of all consolation." 2 Corinthians 1:3

"Devote yourselves to prayer, keeping alert in it with thanksgiving." Colossians 4:2

Thought for today: Thanksgiving to God should be every day, not just one single Thursday per year.

Story 28 - St. Joseph's Altar

St. Joseph's day is celebrated on March 19th every year. The "St. Joseph Altar" is an old tradition from Sicily that started when a rain shortage was ruining the crops. The people prayed to St. Joseph for rain, and when it came, they rejoiced and prepared a table of food that they had harvested, and shared the food with those less fortunate*.

My grandparents prayed to St. Joseph that their two sons would come back safely from World War II. When they did return, my grandparents decided that they would make a St. Joseph's altar in their home every year. They would prepare special foods, and neighbors would bring their own special foods over and add to the altar in the house. On St. Joseph's day, my grandfather and aunt would drive their cars over to the local orphanage in Birmingham, Alabama, and pick up 10 or 11 orphans and bring them to their home for a luncheon feast. The orphans, along with one or two of the grandkids, would sit around a large table in the dining room and be fed all that they could eat. Each child at the table would be given the name of one of the twelve apostles, reminding us of the Last Supper. After these twelve had eaten, then the rest of the family could then eat what was left over. (It was tough waiting outside the door until about 1pm to eat, especially when all that food was putting out such a great aroma!)

After the orphans had their fill, they would be taken back to the orphanage to talk about those "crazy Italians" that had just fed them a great meal. The St. Joseph altar traditions continue in many parts of the world, and have been embraced by people of other nationalities. It can be a source of new requests and thanksgiving for prayers answered.

---

* See additional information at "History of the St. Joseph Altar" at CatholicCulture.org.

THANKSGIVING

By giving thanks to God, you will experience joy. He truly wants you to be happy.

<u>Be thankful that God loved you enough to send His only Son to save your soul.</u>

Be thankful to Jesus for dying for you. He cares for you that much.

God knows all of your troubles and worries. Thank Him for the strength to carry on.

Be thankful for all the blessings that God has showered on you. Whatever you have, big or small, are all special gifts from Him.

Be thankful for each family member and friend that you have. Each one was carefully picked out *just for you.*

Take some time each Sunday (or any other day), to thank God for all that has happened to you in the past week. *The good things should make you smile, and the bad things should make you stronger.*

When is the best time to give thanks? How about *right now*!

Prayer: Dear God, I give you thanks for all of the blessings that You have bestowed on me and my family.

Topic: **THANKSGIVING**   REFLECTION   Date: _____

Which messages spoke to you on this topic? Underline words or sentences that touched you. Then write down what else came to your mind because of these words:

_____

1. _____

_____

2. _____

_____

3. _____

_____

4. _____

_____

5. _____

_____

Now, write down <u>what you intend to do today or this week</u>, to answer these messages:

_____

1. _____

_____

2. _____

_____

3. _____

_____

4. _____

_____

5. _____

_____

25) TRUST

"Surely God is my salvation; I will trust, and will not be afraid, for the Lord God is my strength and my might; He has become my salvation." Isaiah 12:2

"Trust in the Lord, and do good; so you will live in the land, and enjoy security." Psalm 37:3

"Moreover, it is required of stewards that they be found trustworthy." 1 Corinthians 4:2

Thought for today: You can trust Jesus. Can He also trust you?

Story 29 - Letting Go

It was 1995. I had been laid off from my job, and couldn't find another one. After six months, I was running out of money and had to be out of my apartment by the end of the month. I sold my furniture to buy food. I was sleeping on the floor. My car broke down and I couldn't get it fixed. I had tried everything on my own and nothing was working. A friend had given me a St. Jude prayer card, the "patron of hopeless causes"-and that I certainly was. One night I broke down after praying to St. Jude and I let go of everything. I remember praying: "OK God, I have done all that I can. There is nothing more I can humanly do; I am letting go and letting You take over my life completely".

The very next morning, I got a phone call from the State Employment Office asking me if I would be interested in interviewing for a job as a teacher for the Birmingham City Schools. I would need to interview with the principal of a high school that was starting a TV Production program, and I was the only person in the State database that had TV production experience.

At the interview the principal liked me and said I would have to start next week. It turned out that one of my best friends also taught at the same high school. He said that I could move in with him and his family until I could get back on my feet financially, and I could ride to work with him every day until I could get my car fixed. I stayed with them for four months until I was able to get my own apartment.

In addition to this new direction God had laid out for me, He also helped me fulfill a dream I had always had about going to Hollywood to see the movie business firsthand. I knew that I could never afford it-but it turned out that the same high school started an animation program, where they worked online with animators from Hollywood. So for a few years I got an all-expense paid trip as one of the chaperones for these students as they attended summer workshops in Hollywood and toured the movie studios!

In September of 1995, I attended a Cursillo retreat weekend, and at an Ultreya retreat event a couple of years later I was asked to share my faith journey with the members. The date of my talk was October 28th-*St. Jude's Feast Day.*

Kevin Smith
Birmingham, AL.

TRUST

Do you know what "joyful trust" is? It is being happy knowing that whatever you cannot control in your life is a blessing from God. So even your bad days and crosses can be gifts that bring you closer to Him.

Jesus wants you to *trust Him* and *thank Him* daily. These actions are so small compared to the gifts that you and I are given each day.

"Come quickly to help me, my Lord and my salvation." (Psalm 37:16)

Trust in Jesus and hold His hand. He will never let go of yours.

If you believe, you must trust. If you trust, you will find peace.

Tithe to your church and other charities. Trust that God will take care of you and your family.

Trust in God's plan for you. Move forward with joyful action.

Remember, nothing that will happen to you today is by accident. <u>And nothing is going to happen to you today that you and Jesus can't handle.</u>

Prayer: I will joyfully trust in God today.

Topic: **TRUST** _____ REFLECTION   Date: _____

Which messages spoke to you on this topic? Underline words or sentences that touched you. Then write down what else came to your mind because of these words:

_____

1. _____

_____

2. _____

_____

3. _____

_____

4. _____

_____

5. _____

_____

Now, write down <u>what you intend to do today or this week</u>, to answer these messages:

_____

1. _____

_____

2. _____

_____

3. _____

_____

4. _____

_____

5. _____

_____

26) WORRY

"Therefore I tell you, do not worry about your life, what you will eat or what you will drink, or about your body, what you will wear. Is not life more than food, and the body more than clothing?" Matthew 6:25

"Do not worry about anything, but in everything by prayer and supplication with thanksgiving let your requests be made known to God." Philippians 4:6

"And can any of you by worrying add a single hour to your span of life?" Matthew 6:27

Thought for today: Worry and fear are useless. What is needed is trust in God and in His Son, Jesus.

Story 30 - Comforting Message

My wife's mother died suddenly from a heart attack in Atlanta in 2006. My wife was sad that she did not get to talk to her mother at least one more time, as we all have been when a loved one dies without a warning.

After a long day of notifying relatives and friends, we finally were able to get to bed. I had a dream about my mother-in-law that night. She appeared to me and said to "tell everyone that I am alright, and not to worry".

Sometimes God uses us to bring messages of consolation to others who are suffering. Be on the lookout for things that happen to you today, that might enable you to be a "comforter to others". It might not be through something as remarkable as a dream, but it may be a kind word or smile that could bring hope or joy to someone in need.

WORRY

As Mark Twain once said: "I have lived through some terrible things in my life, some of which actually happened." (goodreads.com)

Also, Will Rogers said: "Worrying is like paying on a debt that may never come due." (brainyquote.com)

God does not want me to worry. Repeat that sentence several times.

We are all concerned about our health, livelihood, kids, parents, relatives, and friends. But many times we worry too much and this could be a sign of a lack of faith. Take some time each day to sit quietly asking God to help you not to worry. He is always watching and knows what is going to happen to you.

Worry doesn't prevent things from happening, but it can make things worse.

Too much worrying is bad for your physical and spiritual health. Don't waste precious time by being concerned about what *has* happened in your past, or what *may* happen tomorrow.

Today is a new day, so *strive to live in the present moment,* which is all that we really can control. Jesus said: "So do not worry about tomorrow, for tomorrow will bring worries of its own. Today's trouble is enough for today." (Mt. 6:34)

Stop now and pray; you will accomplish much more today.

Try having one day per week where you do not worry, but allow God to take over. Start with a "Worry-Free Friday". After a few weeks, add another day, and then another. Pretty soon, you may be on your way to a "Worry-Free Life"!

God made you to live with Him for all eternity in peace and happiness, without worry or fear. Thank Him daily for this great plan!

Prayer: Heavenly Father, teach me not to worry. You hold me in the palm of Your loving hand.

Topic: **WORRY** _____ REFLECTION   Date: _____

Which messages spoke to you on this topic? Underline words or sentences that touched you. Then write down what else came to your mind because of these words:

_____

1. _____

_____

2. _____

_____

3. _____

_____

4. _____

_____

5. _____

_____

Now, write down <u>what you intend to do today or this week</u>, to answer these messages:

_____

1. _____

_____

2. _____

_____

3. _____

_____

4. _____

_____

5. _____

_____

_____

Summary

This workbook is an attempt to get you (or keep you) on the pathway to heaven.

My goal is to give you a message of hope and a daily outline to keep you moving forward to your eternal destiny. Use this heavenly formula:

Trust Jesus + Thank Jesus + Love Jesus + Perform good works = Eternity in heaven.

If you follow the above formula, there is no need for fear, anger, or anxiety.

I believe that the majority (if not all) of these thoughts were given to me by the Holy Spirit, as I was in Church before the tabernacle, or at the Adoration of Jesus in the Catholic form of the Eucharistic Host, when most of this book was written.

If any of these thoughts reach you spiritually, then I am thankful for the opportunity to bring them to you. My sincerest hope is that this simple book will help many people. I will rejoice if you are one of them! Please let me know how this book has affected you by writing to me at the following email address:

heavenlyworkbook1@aol.com

I'll end with this prayer:

Lord, lead me to what makes *You* happy today, so that one day I might share in Your Heavenly Father's home.

God bless you today and forever!

Acknowledgements

Special thanks to my friends for their stories included in this book. Each story has a unique message of how God works in the lives of the faithful. Each writer's individual effort helped me to complete my overall message that: ***God wants each of us to earn a place in heaven.***

Thanks to my friend, Dr. John J. Parrino, for his input and suggestions, as he has written several books and saved me lots of time in this endeavor.

Special thanks to my wife, Mae Beth, for her input and patience in this task of being a messenger.

And finally, special thanks to my sons Adam and Jason, for their computer skills in putting this manuscript together. They helped their "technologically challenged" dad many times, in order to get this book to the finish line.